A Book of Four-Part Madrigals (S.A.T.B.)

CONTENTS

For Editorial Notes see page 53

Oxford University Press
Music Department, 37 Dover Street, London W1X

1
ADIEU, SWEET AMARYLLIS

JOHN WILBYE

Not too fast and with elegance

Printed in Great Britain

6

2
APRIL IS IN MY MISTRESS' FACE

THOMAS MORLEY

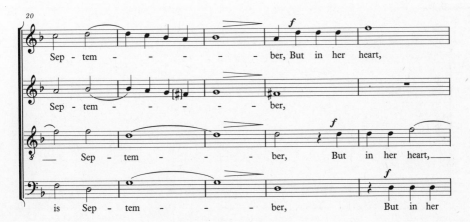

3
CONSTURE MY MEANING

GILES FARNABY

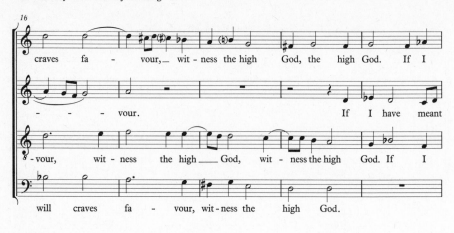

craves fa - vour, _ wit - ness the high God, the high God. If I

- - - vour.   If I have meant

- vour,   wit - ness the high _ God, wit - ness the high God. If I

will craves fa - vour, wit - ness the high God.

have meant well, _ have meant well, if I have meant well, good will re - -

well, good will re - ward, re - ward me, if (I have meant well, good will re -

have meant _ well, meant well, if I have _ meant well, good

If I have meant well, good will re -

- - ward me; When I de - serve ill, no man _ re - gard, no

- ward me;) When I de - serve ill, no man _ re - gard, me,

will re - ward me; When I de - serve ill, no man re - gard _

- ward me; When I de - serve ill, _ no man re -

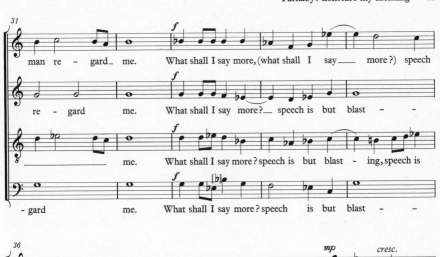

31

man re - gard me. What shall I say more, (what shall I say___ more?) speech

re - gard me. What shall I say more?___ speech is but blast - -

_____ me. What shall I say more? speech is but blast - ing, speech is

- gard me. What shall I say more? speech is but blast - -

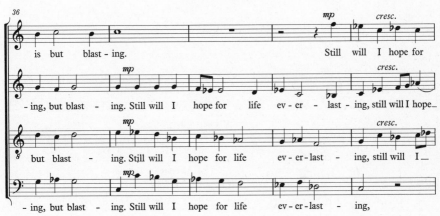

36

is but blast - ing. Still will I hope for

- ing, but blast - ing. Still will I hope for life ev - er - last - ing, still will I hope___

but blast - ing. Still will I hope for life ev - er - last - ing, still will I___

- ing, but blast - ing. Still will I hope for life ev - er - last - ing,

41

life ev - er - last - ing, for life ev - er - last - ing.

___ for life ev - er - last - ing, I hope for life ev - er - last - ing.

hope for life, still will I hope for___ life, hope for life ev - er - last - ing.

still will I hope for life ev - er - last - ing.

4
FAIR PHYLLIS I SAW

JOHN FARMER

5
O YES! HAS ANY FOUND A LAD?

THOMAS TOMKINS

6
WEEP, O MINE EYES

JOHN BENNET

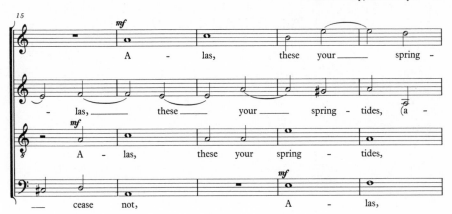

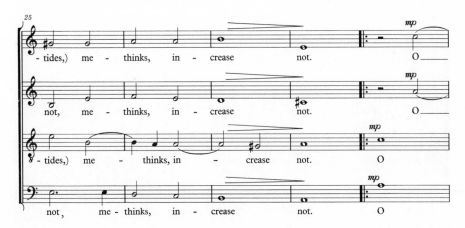

7
ANCOR CHE COL PARTIRE

A. d'Avalos

RORE

8
CHI VUOL' UDIR'

MARENZIO

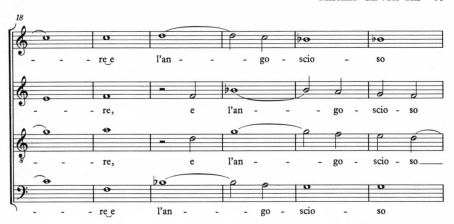

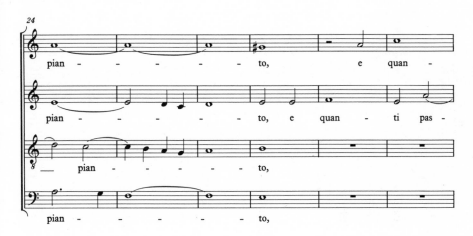

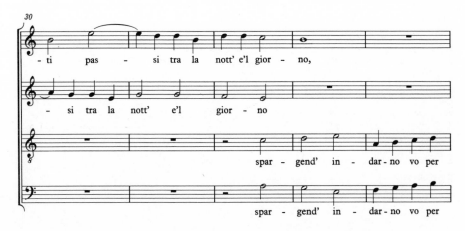

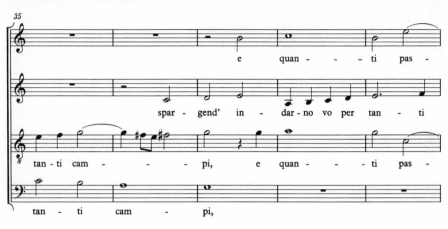

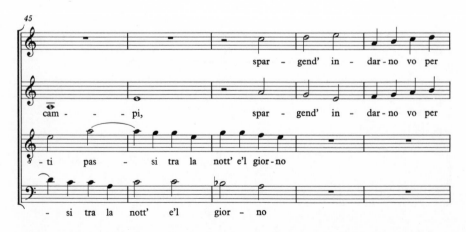

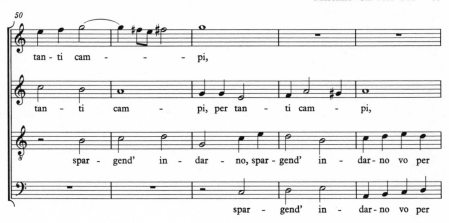

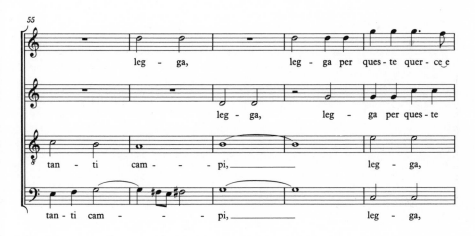

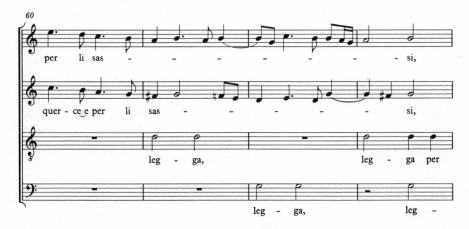

e ____ per li sas - - - si, che n'è già

e per li sas - - - si, che ____ n'è già ____

ques-te quer-ce e per li sas - - - si,

- ga per ques-te quer-ce e per li sas - - - si, che n'è già

pien' o - mai, che n'è già pien' o - mai cia - scu -

____ pien' o - mai, che ____ n'è già ____ pien' o - mai cia -

che n'è già pien' o - mai cia -

pien' o - mai,

- na val - - - le, che n'è già pien' o -

- scu - na val - le, che ____ n'è già ____ pien' o -

- scu - na val - le,

che n'è già pien' o -

9
CHI SALIRÀ PER ME

Ariosto

WERT

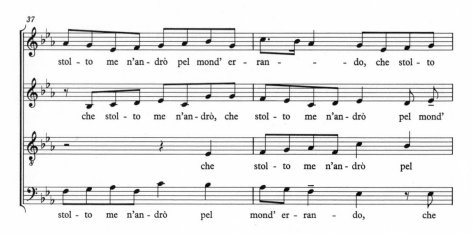

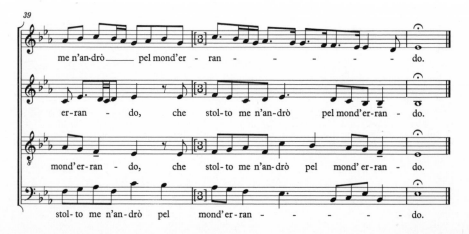

10
IL BIANCO E DOLCE CIGNO

A. d'Avalos

ARCADELT

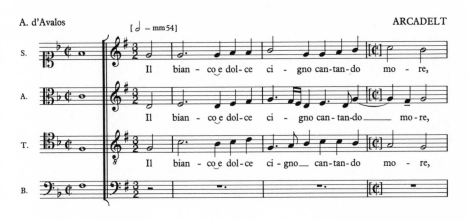

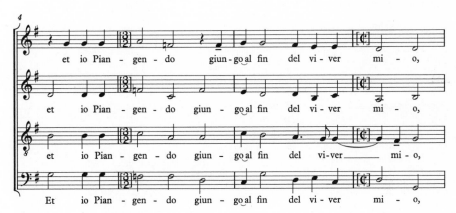

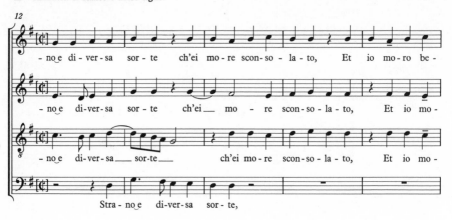

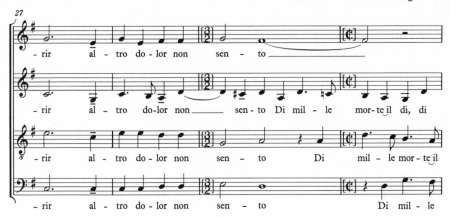

11
IO MI SON GIOVINETTA

Boccaccio

D. M. FERRABOSCO

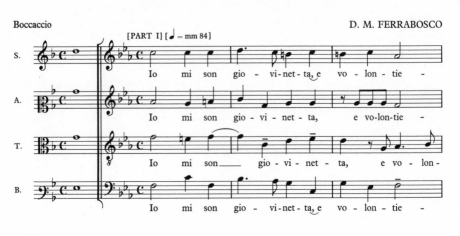

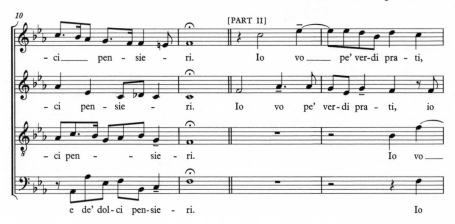

[PART II]

-ci___ pen - sie - ri.   Io   vo___ pe' ver-di pra - ti,

-ci pen - sie - ri.   Io   vo   pe' ver-di pra - ti,   io

-ci pen - - sie - ri.   Io   vo___

e de' dol-ci pen-sie - ri.   Io

io   vo pe' ver - di pra - ti ri - guar -

vo pe' ver-di pra - - ti   ri - guar -

pe' ver-di pra - ti,   io   vo pe' ver - di

vo   pe' ver-di pra - ti   ri - guar -

-dan - - - do I bian-chi fio - ri,   i

-dan - - - do I bian-chi fio - ri,   i bian-chi

pra - ti ri-guar-dan - do   I bian-chi fio - ri, e' gial - li,

-dan - - - do   I bian-chi fio -

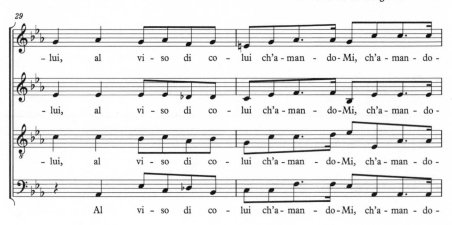

12
TUTTO LO DÌ

LASSUS

S.

Tut - to lo di, tut - to lo di, tut - to lo di mi
di - ci: can - ta,_____ can - ta. Non ve - di ca non pos - so, non
ve - di ca non pos - so re - fia - ta - re. A_____

A.

Tut - to lo di, tut - to lo di, tut - to lo di mi
di - ci: can - ta, can - ta. Non ve - di ca non pos - so, non
ve - di ca non pos - so re - fia - ta - re. A che

T.

Tut - to lo di, tut - to lo di, tut - to lo di mi
di - ci: can - ta, can - ta. Non ve - di ca non pos - so, non
ve - di ca non pos - so re - fia - ta - re. A_____ che tan -

B.

Tut - to lo di, tut - to lo di, tut - to lo di mi
di - ci: can - ta, can - ta. Non ve - di ca non pos - so, non
ve - di ca non pos - so re - fia - ta - re. A_____ che tan -

Editorial Notes

A. English Madrigals (Nos. 1–6)

Nos. 1–6 are taken from *The Oxford Book of English Madrigals* edited by Philip Ledger, with a critical commentary by Andrew Parker (OUP 1978).

EDITORIAL METHOD

All tempi indications, dynamics, and material in square brackets are editorial. Large accidentals in parentheses are implicit from the conventions of the source or sources but are not notated therein. Small accidentals in parentheses are cautionary. Coloration is denoted by a broken brace round the groups of notes. Where repetition of text in the sources is indicated by *bis* markings, the text is here placed in parentheses.

SOURCES

1. Wilbye: *The First Set Of English Madrigals To 3. 4. 5. and 6. voices,* 1598; British Library Add. MSS 29372-7; Royal College of Music MS 684

2. Morley: *Madrigalls To Fovre Voyces . . . The First Booke,* 1594; British Library Add. MS 15117 (voice and lute), Add. MS 36484 (iv only)

3. Farnaby: *Canzonets To Fowre Voyces,* 1598

4. Farmer: *The First Set Of English Madrigals: To Foure Voices,* 1599

5. Tomkins: *Songs Of 3. 4. 5. and 6. parts,* 1622

6. Bennet: *Madrigalls To Fovre Voyces,* 1599

A list of variants and fuller details of sources are provided in *The Oxford Book of English Madrigals.*

B. Italian Madrigals (Nos. 7, 9, 10, 11)

Nos. 7, 9, 10, 11 are taken from *The Oxford Book of Italian Madrigals* edited by Alec Harman (OUP 1983).

EDITORIAL METHOD

Material in square brackets and small accidentals are editorial. Double-bars and repeat dots are editorial, passages being written out in full in the originals. In order to assist singers to accentuate correctly, the following points, some being modifications of accepted practice, should be studied:

1. In homorhythmic passages where all or most of the voices are, in effect, in triple metre, though still governed by '₵' or 'C', the number '3' in square brackets is used to denote $\frac{3}{4}\binom{6}{8}$ or $\frac{3}{2}\binom{6}{4}$, depending on the context. But in certain cases, for the sake of clarity, the actual time signature (in square brackets) is given.

2. The first minim in a bar in '₵', and the first and third crotchets in 'C', are accented, unless preceded or succeeded by a longer note (or the equivalent in shorter note-values), including tied notes, or by a note with a stress mark (—).

3. The first quaver in a group of two is accented unless preceded by an accented note or a quaver rest.

4. The third quaver in a group of four is accented.

5. The first quaver in a group of three is accented unless preceded by a quaver rest or a dotted crotchet.

6. A single quaver is unaccented.

7. The stress mark is used for exceptions to, or instances not covered by, the above.

8. Generally speaking, the accent in Italian is on the penultimate syllable if the word ends in a vowel (am*o*re), and on the final syllable if the word ends with a consonant or an accented vowel (mor*ir*, piet*à*).

SOURCES

7. *Musica Divina*, 1583

9. *First book of madrigals a 4*, 1583

10. *First book of madrigals a 4*, 1539

11. *Musica Divina*, 1583

TRANSLATIONS

The translations of Nos. 7 and 11 are by H. E. Smither and
A. Illiano in A. Einstein's *The Italian Madrigal*, Vol. III and are
reproduced by permission. Thanks are due to Anna Bartrum for
providing the translation of No. 9 and checking that of No. 10.

7. Although when I depart/ I feel myself dying,/ To part I would
like always, at every moment,/ So great is the pleasure that I feel/
From the life I gain on coming back./ And thus thousands of times
a day/ To part from you I would like,/ So sweet is my returning.

9. Who will ascend for me, my Lady, to heaven/ To bring back my
lost reason/ Which, since departed from your beautiful eyes the
dart/ That my heart pierced, every hour I am losing?/ Nor of such a
loss do I complain,/ Provided it increases not, but remains at this
degree;/ For I doubt, if more it diminishes,/ That foolish I shall go
through the world wandering.

10. The white and gentle swan dies singing, and I/ Weeping reach
the end of my life./ What strange and diverse fate that he dies
unconsoled,/ And I die blessed./ Death, which in dying/ Fills me
full of joy and desire./ If in dying no other pain I feel/ With a
thousand deaths a day I would be content.

11. I am a young lady, and gladly/ Rejoice and sing in the new
season,/ Thanks to love and to my sweet thoughts./ I go through
green meadows looking/ At the white flowers, the yellow and red,/
The roses above their thorns, and white lilies,/ And all of these I go
on comparing/ To the face of him in whose love/ I was taken and
will be held forever.

C. Italian Madrigals (Nos. 8 and 12)

No. 8 is taken from *Marenzio: Ten Madrigals* edited by Denis Arnold (OUP 1966).

EDITORIAL METHOD
Small accidentals and bar-lines are editorial.

SOURCE
Madrigali a quattro voci, Venice, 1585, Gardano. Verse: from Sannazaro's *Arcadia*

TRANSLATION
The translation is by the editor.
8. He who would hear of my sighs in verse, my dear ladies, and of my anguished plaint, and of how many steps both night and day I tread in vain in many meadows, let him regard these oak trees and these rocks, for each valley is full of my weeping.

No. 12 is taken from *Orlandus Lassus: Ten Madrigals* edited by Denis Arnold (OUP 1977).

EDITORIAL METHOD
Small accidentals, material in square brackets, and bar-lines are editorial.

SOURCE
Libro de Villanelle Moresche et altre canzoni à 4, 5, 6, & 8 voci, Paris 1581, le Roy & Ballard

TRANSLATION
The translation is by Dr Barbara Reynolds.
12. All day long you bid me sing, sing. Do you not see I am out of breath? What is the use of all this singing? I wish you would bid me ring, not the bells at nones, but your cymbal. Ah, if I live, hey, nonny, no, let me but hold you in my clutches.